Bugs Are Beautiful!

A+ books®

BREATHTAKING Beetles

by Catherine Ipcizade

Consultant:
Laura Jesse
Director, Plant and Insect Diagnostic Clinic
Iowa State University Extension
Ames, Iowa

• • •

CAPSTONE PRESS
a capstone imprint

A+ Books are published by Capstone Press
1710 Roe Crest Drive, North Mankato, Minnesota 56003
www.mycapstone.com

Library of Congress Cataloging-in-Publication Data
Names: Ipcizade, Catherine, author.
Title: Breathtaking beetles / by Catherine Ipcizade.
Description: North Mankato, Minnesota : Capstone Press, [2017] | Series: A+ books. Bugs are beautiful |
Audience: Ages 4-8. | Audience: K to grade 3.
  | Includes bibliographical references and index.
Identifiers: LCCN 2016032391 (print) | LCCN 2016038723 (ebook) | ISBN
  9781515744979 (library binding) | ISBN 9781515745013 (pbk.) | ISBN
  9781515745136 (eBook PDF)
Subjects: LCSH: Beetles–Juvenile literature.
Classification: LCC QL576.2 .I63 2017 (print) | LCC QL576.2 (ebook) | DDC 595.76–dc23
LC record available at https://lccn.loc.gov/2016032391

Editorial Credits

Editor, Abby Colich; Designer, Bobbie Nuytten; Media Researcher, Jo Miller; Production Specialist, Tori Abraham

Photo Credits

Alamy: blickwinkel, cover, blickwinkel/Kottmann, 11, Graphic Science, 19, imageBROKER/Alexandra Laube,
23, Robert Shantz, 9; Dreamstime: Galinasavina, 10; Minden Pictures: Mitsuhiko Imamori, 30 (molt), MYN/
John Tiddy, 17, Nature Production/Kazuo Unno, 20; Newscom: Minden Pictures/Mark Moffett, 24, Minden
Pictures/Thomas Marent, 14, Photoshot/NHPA/Robert Pickett, 12; Science Source: James H. Robinson, 30 (eggs,
larva, pupa, adult), Stuart Wilson, 8; Shutterstock: A.S.Floro, 26, Cosmin Manci, 27, Dennis van de Water, 22,
EarnestTse, 5 (bottom left), Imladris, 4, Katarina Christenson, 16, khlongwangchao, 5 (top), Liew Weng Keong, 25,
macrowildlife, 7, Nicola Dal Zotto, 21, Paolo Costa, 1, photowind, 28, Puwadol Jaturawutthichai, map (throughout),
RODINA OLENA, back cover (background), Sarah2, 6, seiyoh, 15, Trifecta, 18, TTstudio, 29, Weblogiq, 5 (bottom
right); SuperStock: agf photo, 13

Note to Parents, Teachers, and Librarians

This Bugs Are Beautiful book uses full-color photographs and a nonfiction
format to introduce the concept of beetles. Bugs Are Beautiful is designed
to be read aloud to a pre-reader or to be read independently by an early
reader. Photographs help listeners and early readers understand the text and
concepts discussed. The book encourages further learning by including the
following sections: Table of Contents, Glossary, Read More, Internet Sites,
Critical Thinking Questions Using the Common Core, and Index. Early readers
may need assistance using these features.

Printed and bound in China.
007882

Table of Contents

A colorful insect sits on a flower. Its shiny wings open wide. It flies away. Another insect scurries by. It can't fly. But it is bright and colorful. These insects are beetles.

Some, but not all, beetles are dull and brown. Others are bright colors. They have fun patterns. Some are shiny. Beetles truly are breathtaking.

Bee Beetle

RANGE: Europe

LENGTH: 0.4 inches (1 centimeter)

BREATHTAKING FEATURE: Looks like a bee

Look at that black and yellow bug! It is fuzzy too. It is sitting on a flower. Is it a bee? Look again! This bug is a beetle. Why does it look like a bee? Some animals mimic other animals. They may do this to protect themselves. A predator might think this beetle is a stinging bee. It stays away.

Blue Fungus Beetle

RANGE: Parts of the United States, northern Mexico

LENGTH: 0.6 inches (1.5 cm)

BREATHTAKING COLOR: Blue or purple

It's a blue bug! The blue fungus beetle also has black dots on its body. This bug lives in forests. Females lay eggs on rotting wood. Black and white larvae hatch. They feast on fungus that grows nearby. Adults eat fungus too. Fungus is this beetle's favorite food!

Checkered Beetle

RANGE: Parts of Canada and the United States

LENGTH: 0.6 inches (1.5 cm)

BREATHTAKING FACT: Lays eggs in beehives

Can a beetle look like a checkerboard? The checkered beetle does! It is black with bright red bands. It is hairy too! What else is interesting about this bug? It lays eggs in beehives. Larvae hatch from the eggs. Then the larvae eat the bees' eggs and larvae. As adults, these beetles eat pollen from flowers.

Domino Beetle

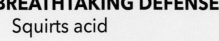

RANGE: India

LENGTH: 1.6 inches (4 cm)

BREATHTAKING DEFENSE:
Squirts acid

What game piece does this bug look like? A domino! The domino beetle lives in deserts and other dry areas. It uses long legs to run quickly. Its legs also raise its body away from hot sand. How does this beetle protect itself? By squirting acid! Predators nearby should watch out.

Eupholus **Weevils**

RANGE: New Guinea

LENGTH: 1.3 inches (3.2 cm)

BREATHTAKING COLORS:
Bright blues and greens

Look at this bright bug! Eupholus weevils come in shades of blue and green. The colors warn predators to stay away. Most eupholus weevils eat yam leaves. The leaves are toxic to other animals.

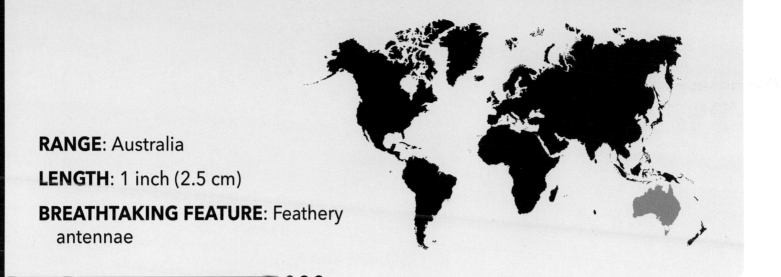

RANGE: Australia

LENGTH: 1 inch (2.5 cm)

BREATHTAKING FEATURE: Feathery
antennae

Are those feathers? No! They are the feather-horned beetle's antennae. Males use the antennae to track a female's scent. But there is more to see on this bug. It has dark grey or black wings. The wings are covered with white dots. Its underside is covered with hair!

antenna

Fiddler Beetle

Look at this bug's markings. Do you see the shape of a fiddle or violin? The fiddler beetle doesn't play music. But it sure looks stunning! Its home is rotting wood. When larvae hatch, they eat the wood. Adults feast on pollen and nectar from flowers.

RANGE: Australia

LENGTH: 0.8 inches (2 cm)

BREATHTAKING FEATURE: Yellow or green markings

RANGE: Southeast Asian Islands

LENGTH: 2 inches (5 cm)

BREATHTAKING FEATURE: Legs that look like a frog's

Is that a tiny frog? No. It's the frog-legged beetle. Its hind legs look like a frog's. But this bug doesn't jump. It climbs plant stems. Tiny hairs on its legs help it hold on tightly. What is even more breathtaking? This beetle's bright green color seems to change in the light.

Giraffe **Weevil**

RANGE: Madagascar

LENGTH: 1 inch (2.5 cm)

BREATHTAKING FEATURE: Long neck

Whoa! Look at that neck! A male giraffe weevil's neck is longer than its body. Males stick out their necks and fight one another. Females have shorter necks. They use their necks to make nests. They roll up a leaf into a tube. Then they lay an egg inside.

beetle after mating

What is that shiny bug? It's the golden tortoise beetle! This tiny bug is smaller than a pea. Its gold body is flecked with small dots. Some people call it "goldbug." When the beetle mates, it changes color. It turns red, brown, or orange. It may even get black spots!

RANGE: North and South America

LENGTH: 0.3 inches (0.7 cm)

BREATHTAKING COLOR: Gold

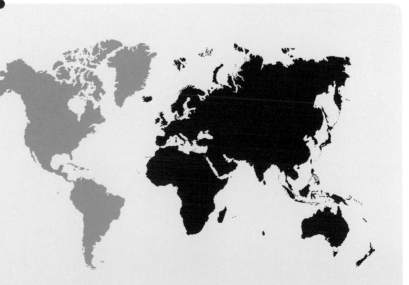

Jewel Beetles

This bug is a gem! The jewel beetle sparkles in the light. It is also called the metallic wood-boring beetle. It lives in forests. Adults feast on plant leaves, pollen, and nectar. Larvae eat dead or dying wood.

RANGE: Worldwide

LENGTH: Up to 3.2 inches (8 cm)

BREATHTAKING FEATURE: Sparkles in light

antennae

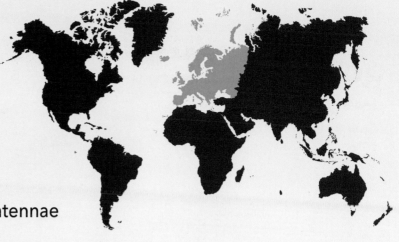

RANGE: Europe

LENGTH: 1.5 inches (3.8 cm)

BREATHTAKING FEATURE: Long antennae

Are those horns? No! They are the rosalia longicorn's antennae. A male's antennae can be longer than its body. Check out those black stripes on the antennae. They are actually hair!

Chirp! This beetle makes noise when it rubs its legs and wings together.

hair

Life Cycle of a Beetle

1. Beetles begin life as eggs.

2. A larva hatches from an egg.

3. A larva molts as it grows.

4. A larva forms a pupa.

5. An adult emerges from the pupa.

Glossary

antenna (an-TE-nuh)—a feeler on an insect's head

feature (FEE-chur)—an important part or quality of something

fungus (FUHN-guhs)—a type of organism that has no leaves, flowers, or roots

larva (LAR-vuh)—an insect at a stage of development between egg and adult

mate (MATE)—to join together to produce young

mimic (MIM-ik)—to imitate the look, actions, or behaviors of another plant or animal

molt (MOLT)—to shed the hard outer covering while growing

nectar (NEK-tur)—a sweet liquid that some insects collect from flowers and eat as food

pollen (POL-uhn)—tiny, yellow grains in flowers

predator (PRED-uh-tur)—an animal that hunts another animal for food

range (RAYNJ)—an area where an animal mostly lives

toxic (TOK-sik)—poisonous

Read More

Long, Erin. *Ground Beetles*. Dig Deep! Bugs That Live Underground. New York: PowerKids Press, 2016.

Polinsky, Paige V. *Rhinoceros Beetle: Heavyweight Champion*. Animal Superstars. Minneapolis: Abdo Publishing, 2016.

Rissman, Rebecca. *Beetles*. Creepy Critters. Chicago: Raintree, 2013.

Internet Sites

FactHound offers a safe, fun way to find Internet sites related to this book. All of the sites on FactHound have been researched by our staff.

Here's all you do:

Visit *www.facthound.com*

Type in this code: 9781515744979

Super-cool stuff! Check out projects, games and lots more at **www.capstonekids.com**

Critical Thinking Using the Common Core

1. Why do some animals mimic other animals? (Key Idea and Details)

2. Page 15 says yam leaves are toxic. Use the glossary on page 31 to define toxic. (Craft and Structure)

3. Choose two beetles from the book. How are they alike? How are they different? (Integration of Knowledge and Ideas)

Index